FOREST FIRE

by

Dougal Dixon

WATERBIRD BOOKS

Columbus, Ohio

EXPEDITION EARTH

FOREST
FIRE

by Dougal Dixon

McGraw Hill Children's Publishing

© ticktock Entertainment Ltd. 2004

First published in Great Britain in 2004 by ticktock Media Ltd.,

Unit 2, Orchard Business Centre, North Farm Road, Tunbridge Wells, Kent, TN2 3XF

We would like to thank David Gillingwater and Elizabeth Wiggans

Illustrations by John Alston and David Gillingwater

This edition published in the United States of America in 2004 by

Waterbird Books, an imprint of

McGraw-Hill Children's Publishing,

a Division of the McGraw-Hill Companies

8787 Orion Place

Columbus, Ohio 43240-4027

www.MHkids.com

Library of Congress Cataloging-in-Publication Data is on file with the publisher.

t=top, b=bottom, c=center, l=left, r=right, OFC=outside front cover, OBC=outside back cover

Alamy images: OFCl, 3b, 4tr, 5tl, 10tr, 11b, 12tr, 14tr, 14br, 16br, 20cb, 24br, 26tr, 26b. Corbis: OFCbr, 4tc, 6tr, 6-7c, 7tl, 8tr, 8bc, 8-9b, 9cr, 10-11c, 11tr, 12cr, 12-13, 15tr, 16-17c, 19cr, 23c, 26-27c, 28-29c, 29cl. Heritage Images: 9t.

Popperfoto: 22tr. Science Photo Library: 22cr, 24tr, .

Every effort has been made to trace the copyright holders, and we apologize in advance for any unintentional omissions. We would be pleased to insert the appropriate acknowledgements in any subsequent edition of this publication.

Printed in China

1-57768-849-X

1 2 3 4 5 6 7 8 9 10 TTM 09 08 07 06 05 04

CONTENTS

Fascinated By Fire..4

Day 2: Case Study: The Great Barbecue..........6

Day 3: Case Study: The Yellowstone Story.....8

Day 4: Meet the Fire Chief.................................10

Day 4: The Fire Starts 12

Day 4: Fighting Fire With Fire...........................14

Day 5: The Plan...16

Day 5: The Infantry Advance.............................18

Day 5: The Heavy Artillery.................................20

Day 5: Regroup...22

Day 6: Setback..24

Day 7: To the Rescue..26

News Report: A Town Recovers........................28

Glossary...30

Index...32

Elaine Wilkie

DAY 1
Location: *Upper Town*

Hi, I'm Elaine Wilkie. I am doing a feature about wildfires—forest fires and brush fires—for my class project. Right now, I am on spring break, visiting my cousin Albert, who lives in Upper Town. Upper Town is an area that has had trouble with forest fires in the past.

Last week, Albert's uncle, the local fire chief, stopped by. When he heard about my interest in wildfires, he invited me to come to the fire department to see his team in action.

I have to find out as much as I can about wildfires before I go to the firehouse. I've already learned that there are different kinds of wildfires. Forest fires occur in high latitudes, in places like Canada, the northeastern U.S., and Siberia. Brush fires usually occur in places like California, Chile, South Africa, southern Australia, and the Mediterranean countries. Grass fires occur on savannahs and prairies, where it is frequently dry.

This is Smokey Bear, a mascot that has served for almost 50 years to remind people of the importance of outdoor fire safety and wildfire prevention.

WORD MUDDLE

When something is called *inflammable*, it means that it is capable of burning (it can catch fire or "inflame.") In the 1970s, some people thought the word meant that the item was not capable of burning. To prevent a mix-up, the word *flammable* was introduced. Both words are still used today.

This poster is from my favorite film, *Backdraft*.

TRIANGLE OF FIRE

Three conditions must exist before a fire can ignite. First, there must be fuel, or something to burn. Second, there must be oxygen. Finally, there must be heat. Once a fire is cooled below what is called its *ignition temperature* or its *flashpoint*, it will not burn. To control the flames, firefighters attempt to deprive the fire of fuel, heat, or oxygen.

BACKDRAFT

GUIDE TO WILDFIRES

THIS MAP SHOWS AREAS ACROSS THE WORLD AT A RISK OF WILDFIRES

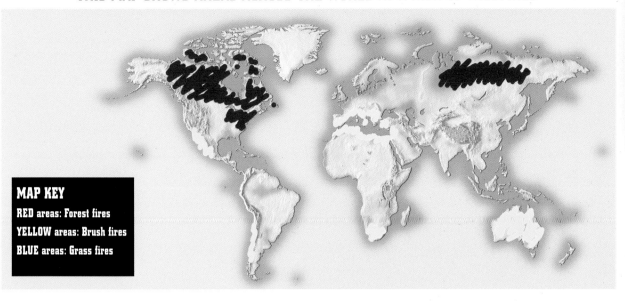

MAP KEY
RED areas: Forest fires
YELLOW areas: Brush fires
BLUE areas: Grass fires

HABITATS

Brush fires occur in dry areas across the world. These areas are found in regions that have sub-tropical climates. In these regions, it is warm and wet with westerly winds in the winter, and hot and dry in the summer.

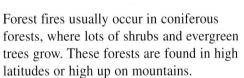

Mediterranean scrub

Conifer forests

Forest fires usually occur in coniferous forests, where lots of shrubs and evergreen trees grow. These forests are found in high latitudes or high up on mountains.

Grass fires are common in natural grasslands. Grass is able to withstand the frequent fires because only the small leaves of the plants burn, leaving the underground stems unharmed.

African grassland

Incoming text... ✉ ▮ ◀

Hi, Elaine.
This is the fire chief. Come to my office in two days, and you'll get a chance to see exactly what we do here. The local meteorologists tell me that the area is at a high risk of forest fires this spring, so be prepared for anything.

SX56

DAY 2
Location: *Town Library*

I am at the library finding out all about some of the most terrible fires that have ever happened. In the fall of 1871, one of the world's deadliest fires took place in Wisconsin. The weather had been very hot with no rain for 14 weeks. On October 8, fires broke out all over the Midwest. The Great Chicago Fire was one of these fires, killing 250 people. It is the most well-known fire because it happened in such a large city. The most serious loss of life occurred in the forested areas of Wisconsin. It was estimated that 1,500 people died that night, and 4.25 million acres of forest were destroyed. It is sometimes called the *Peshtigo Fire*. Reverend Peter Pernin was living in Peshtigo, Wisconsin when the town was destroyed by fire. He wrote a vivid eyewitness account of the blazes. The fire is most commonly known as "The Great Barbecue."

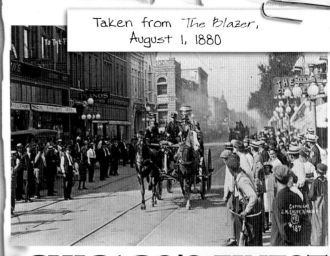

Taken from *The Blazer*, August 1, 1880

CHICAGO'S FINEST

The firefighting equipment used in 1871 was too primitive to battle The Great Chicago Fire. After that, Chicago made several advances in firefighting. The city established a hydrant system, which let firefighters access water through hydrants installed on streets to fight fires. In addition, most firehouses added poles, allowing firefighters to move quickly from the upper level to the lower level of the firehouse during an emergency. Firefighters' hats have also come a long way. The new helmet design caught on across the country and is now known as "the Chicago helmet."

Taken from *The Great Peshtigo Fire: An Eyewitness Account* by Reverend Peter Pernin

EYEWITNESS

"Ever and anon some tall old pine, whose huge trunk had become a column of fire, fell with a thundering crash, filling the air with a cloud of sparks and cinders . . . above this sheet of flames a dense black cloud of resinous smoke seemed to threaten death and destruction to all below."

THE GREAT BARBECUE

CITY LIBRARY
Elaine Wilkie
STUDENT

24532421 243

FIREFIGHTING IN THE 19TH CENTURY

In the 1870s, the most advanced type of firefighting equipment consisted of steam-driven water pumps pulled by horses. In rural areas, though, there was no organized firefighting force. Local companies had to try to mobilize their workers to fight the fire with buckets. People created lines, passing water-filled buckets toward the fire.

FIREFIGHTING TECHNOLOGY

Firefighting technology has improved considerably since the days of The Great Barbecue. Today, coastal cities are patrolled by fireboats that can pump water at high speeds onto harbor fires. The fireboat in this picture is operating around the port city of Seattle.

WISCONSIN TODAY

Wisconsin averages 1,600 fires per year. These fires burn an average of 7,000 acres. The state has a dedicated wildfire fighting service that includes 44 temporary and 45 permanent employees. The employees work with local, state, tribal, and other federal firefighters to control fires. The work one agency does often makes life easier for all the other firefighting agencies. The Wisconsin firefighting team also has seven airtankers that help them to fight fires from the sky.

Wisconsin is proud of its fire service, as shown in this tourist article.

7

DAY 3
Location: *Town Library*

Today, I am learning how park officials and fire-fighters cope with fire in Yellowstone National Park.

There is a long history of wildfire in Yellowstone. Geologists have found evidence of fires that occurred even before written records began in 1872. Geologists gathered the evidence by studying soil profiles, lake sediments, landslides, and ancient trees that had been scarred by fire.

Nearly all of Yellowstone's plant groups have burned at one time or another. Some plant species burn and spread fire more readily than others. In the 1960s and 1970s, firefighters in the park thought it would be better to allow small fires to burn as a natural way of limiting fire damage. In 1988, a huge blaze broke out that could not be controlled. Thousands of acres of woodland were destroyed, and many thousands of animals lost their lives. The disaster shows just how destructive fire can be.

FIRE CONTROL POLICY A SUCCESS

In the 1950s and 1960s, national parks and forests began to experiment with controlled burns, and by the 1970s, Yellowstone and other parks had brought in a natural fire management plan. In the first 16 years of Yellowstone's new fire policy (1972–1987), 235 fires were allowed to burn 33,759 acres. Only 15 of those fires were larger than 100 acres, and all of the fires were extinguished naturally. The public's reaction to the fires was good, and the program was considered a success.

Taken from *The Blazer*, June 10, 1987

ACTIVITY REPORT YELLOWSTONE FIRE

Taken from *The Blazer*, December 21, 1988

FIRE DISASTER HITS YELLOWSTONE

The summer of 1988 turned out to be the driest in the park's recorded history. By July 15, 8,500 acres had burned in the greater Yellowstone area. The dry conditions continued. By July 21, fire activity became noticeable to park visitors, and officials decided to put all fires out. Within a week, fires within the park alone had destroyed nearly 99,000 acres. By the end of the month, dry fuels (trash, plants, and other dry materials) and high winds combined to make the larger fires nearly uncontrollable. National news reporters poured into Yellowstone National Park. Firefighters from around the country and from the army traveled to Yellowstone to help put out the fires.

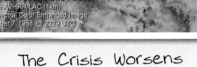

The Great Yellowstone Fires
NOAA-9 AVHRR LAC (1km)
Multi-spectral Color Enhanced Image
September 7, 1988 @ 2229 UTC

The Crisis Worsens

On August 20, 1988, tremendous winds pushed fire across more than 150,000 acres. Throughout August and early September, some park roads and facilities were closed to the public. Residents of nearby towns feared for their property and their lives. Yellowstone's fire management policy was the topic of heated public debate. It was also discussed among members of Congress.

ANIMAL SURVIVORS

Studies showed that 345 elk, 36 deer, 12 moose, 6 black bears, and 9 bison died in greater Yellowstone as a direct result of the fires. Two grizzly bears were missing and were presumed to have also died. Most of the animals that died were trapped as fire quickly swept down two drainage ditches.

DAY 4
Location: *The Fire Station, Upper Town*

I am in the fire chief's office, and he is telling me all about the danger of forest fires in the area. His main job is not to extinguish fires, but to prevent fires from occurring. I've learned that most of the people who work in Upper Town actually live in nearby Lower Town. The community here is growing rapidly, and housing developments are spreading up the hill into the forest. The fire chief is worried that the new houses may now be fireproof, and all the exotic plants in people's lawns and gardens may not be as fire-resistant as the local plants.

The fire department uses a cartoon character named "Sparky the Squirrel" to teach children about the dangers of fire.

The fire chief's cell phone just rang. From the sounds of the fire chief's conversation, I think there may be an emergency.

The fire chief is changing from his uniform into his firefighting gear. He is going out to take a look at the fire so that he can direct operations from the ground.

CAMPFIRES

Follow these tips to make sure you stay safe when building campfires:

- Clear the campfire site and surrounding area.
- Circle the fire pit with rocks.
- Build campfires away from overhanging branches, steep slopes, dry grass, and leaves.
- Keep a bucket of water and a shovel nearby.
- Never leave a campfire unattended.
- To put out a campfire, drown the fire, stir it, and drown it again.
- Always have an adult around to supervise outdoor cooking.
- Be careful with gas lanterns, barbecues, gas stoves, and anything that can start a fire.

Hi, kids.

My name is Sparky the Squirrel. I live in trees, so I know how dangerous forest fires can be. I am here to help you learn to be safe. Nearly all forest fires are started by people. Most people do not intend to start fires. Often, fires are started when people are careless. For this reason, people should obey laws governing fireworks and campfires. Remember, be responsible. You have the power to prevent fires.

KIDS' TIPS
SPARKY SAYS:

- Never play with matches, lighters, flammable liquids, or fire.
- Tell your friends about fire prevention.
- Stay calm during an emergency and listen to instructions from your parents or from another adult who is in charge.

SPARKY'S GUIDE TO FIREWORK SAFETY

If fireworks is permitted in your town, it is important to follow these guidelines:

- Only adults should light fireworks.
- Always read the directions first.
- Never use fireworks near dry grass or other flammable materials.
- Keep a bucket of water and a hose nearby.
- Never attempt to relight or "fix" fireworks.
- Always remember: fireworks are not toys!

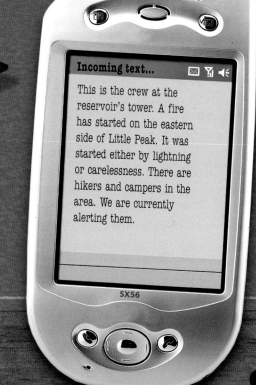

Incoming text... ✉ 📶 🔊

This is the crew at the reservoir's tower. A fire has started on the eastern side of Little Peak. It was started either by lightning or carelessness. There are hikers and campers in the area. We are currently alerting them.

SX56

DAY 4—Late Morning

Location: *The Fire Station, Upper Town*

The fire chief has called in his senior officers to discuss what to do about this new outbreak of fire. I feel like I'm in the way, so I am sitting in a corner of the room taking notes.

There is a big map of the area spread out on the desk. Pilots have radioed details of the fire from their airplanes. It sounds like the fire started near the top of a hill. The hilltops here are covered with dry shrubs, and the valleys have forests of evergreen trees. Both areas are very vulnerable to wildfire.

The firefighters are trying to calculate how the fire will spread before they take action. They are discussing the wind speed and the dryness of the vegetation. The firefighters continue to receive messages about the campsites that are still being evacuated. Currently, there is one group of hikers unaccounted for.

There are not many houses on the side of Little Peak. The houses that do stand on the mountainside are being evacuated as a precautionary measure. Most of the homes are fireproof, but the chief wants to be assured of everyone's safety.

> The fire chief gave me this book that explains how fire spreads. It is easy to see how these disasters start.

THE CANDLE TRICK

We can observe how fires behave in the wind by placing several candles close to one another. In still air, the flame on a lit candle will stay contained to its wick. If there is a draft, the flame will spread from one candle to another. Soon, many of the candles will be burning. Fires that start in forests and woods spread the same way.

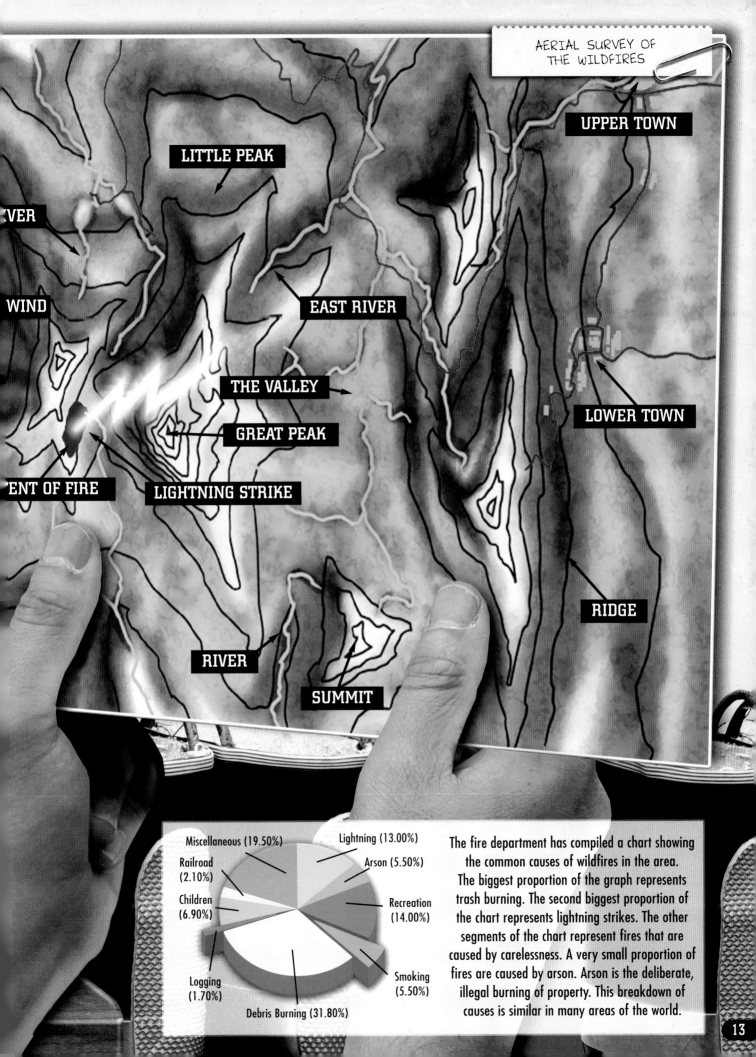

UPPER TOWN

LITTLE PEAK

...VER

WIND

EAST RIVER

THE VALLEY

LOWER TOWN

GREAT PEAK

...ENT OF FIRE

LIGHTNING STRIKE

RIVER

RIDGE

SUMMIT

Miscellaneous (19.50%)

Lightning (13.00%)

Railroad
(2.10%)

Arson (5.50%)

Children
(6.90%)

Recreation
(14.00%)

Logging
(1.70%)

Smoking
(5.50%)

Debris Burning (31.80%)

The fire department has compiled a chart showing
the common causes of wildfires in the area.
The biggest proportion of the graph represents
trash burning. The second biggest proportion of
the chart represents lightning strikes. The other
segments of the chart represent fires that are
caused by carelessness. A very small proportion of
fires are caused by arson. Arson is the deliberate,
illegal burning of property. This breakdown of
causes is similar in many areas of the world.

13

DAY 4—Afternoon
Location: *Below Little Peak*

We have now moved to the area of the fire. It is in a remote location, so we need four-wheel drive vehicles to reach our destination.

The firefighters are beginning to assemble. They have been taken off of their other duties. I've learned that some of their work actually involves lighting fires! Before people lived in this area, firefighters allowed fires that had started naturally from lightning strikes to burn until they extinguished on their own. This process is part of a natural cycle, and it clears away dead plant materials from the ground. Now that there are houses here, the people do not allow natural burning. That means that all kinds of flammable material have collected on the ground and in yards over the years. If a fire does start, it could be very serious.

To counter serious fires, firefighters often start controlled fires to burn off dangerous debris safely. This is what they have been doing this morning.

Firefighters from all over the state are gathering together. They are ready to tackle the blaze if it gets out of control. Firefighters are always ready to move at a moment's notice.

Some firefighters understand fire so thoroughly that they are comfortable being around a blaze that they know is under control. Most confess that they enjoy the challenge.

NEWS REPORT ON CHERNOBYL

In 1986, the atomic power station at Chernobyl in the Ukraine caught fire. It spread radioactive debris over a wide area. The surrounding land was evacuated. Dead plant matter built up on the deserted farmland. Six years later, the land caught fire. Smoke and flying ash carried the contamination even further.

Report taken from *The Blazer*, April 26, 1992

This is a picture that I thought I would never see! Firefighters are actually starting fires. They are conducting a controlled burn to rid the area of flammable undergrowth.

GUIDE TO WILDFIRES

There are different kinds of wildfires.

In a ground fire, the soil burns. Once the fire ignites, the organic matter—peat, partially decayed leaves and twigs, and living roots—burns for a long time. The soil is a good insulator. It retains dangerous the heat, making the fire very difficult to fight.

Surface fires are more common. They occur when fallen branches and undergrowth ignite.

A crown fire burns the tops of the trees. Fire is passed from treetop to treetop in the direction of the wind. The fire may be too high up in the trees for the firefighters to reach it with their fire hoses.

crown fire

surface
fire

ground fire

DAY 5—Morning
Location: *In the Valley*

Rather than rushing in to try to tackle the fire, the firefighters are taking time to come up with a plan. Firefighters have several methods to predict fires. The one that this fire department uses is called the *Campbell Prediction System.* As part of this system, firefighters survey the local area, compiling information about vegetation dryness, the slope of the land (fire burns uphill), and wind direction. From this information, they can pinpoint the areas that will be the most hazardous during a fire. It is incredibly dangerous when a fire reaches a place called the *point of alignment.* At the point of alignment, the ground slope, fuel, and wind conditions are just right to produce an inferno that cannot be controlled.

The first analysis shows that the most vulnerable areas here are on slopes facing west where the vegetation is drying in the afternoon sun. There are two points of alignment here that we must monitor.

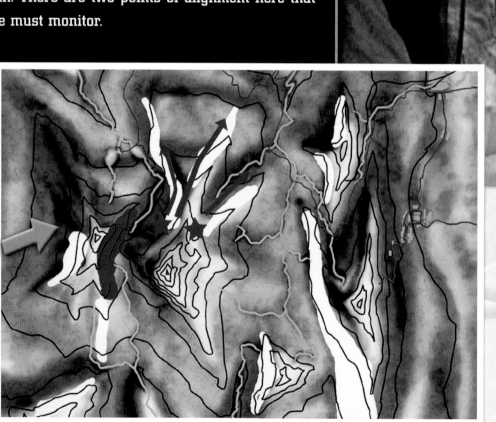

POINTS OF ALIGNMENT
The solid block of red on the situation map shows where the fire is currently burning. The bright yellow patches identify the areas of dry vegetation. The blue arrow is the wind direction. If the fire reaches the points marked by red stars, it will rage out of control in the direction of the red arrows.

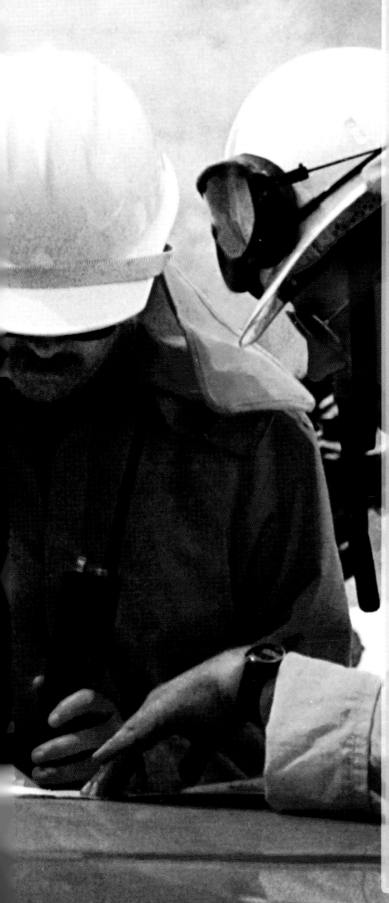

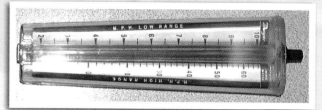

Wind Gauge

The wind gauge is used to determine the strength and direction of the wind. This tool helps the firefighters determine the speed of the fire and the direction in which it is likely to spread.

Fuel Tempometer

The fuel tempometer is an electronic sensor. It estimates the difference in temperature between vegetation in the sunlight and vegetation in the shade. It is used to determine how likely a particular patch of vegetation is to burn.

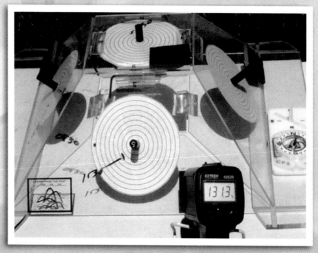

Shadometer

The shadometer is like a sundial. It helps calculate how long the sunlight will fall on a particular area. The longer an area lies in the sunshine, the more likely it is to catch fire.

DAY 5—Afternoon

Location: *Eastern flanks of Little Peak*

The first team of firefighters has gone into action. They have estimated the direction in which the fire is traveling. Along the lower slopes of the hill, the firefighters are using bulldozers and tractors to cut fire breaks in the land. Fire breaks are areas of open ground that are cleared of vegetation. Fire cannot cross these areas.

Farther up the hill, closer to the heart of the fire, smoke jumpers are dropping from airplanes. Smoke jumpers are firefighters who parachute to locations that are difficult to reach. The smoke jumpers will dig trenches and cut back the vegetation by hand. Their mission containing the fire—not putting it out.

There is still no sign of the hikers who are missing. Everybody else has been evacuated from the dangerous areas, and the campsites have been closed. Roadblocks have been set up so that only emergency equipment can get through.

This is one of the firefighters in full uniform.

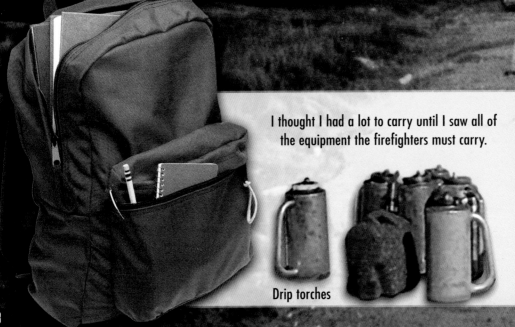

I thought I had a lot to carry until I saw all of the equipment the firefighters must carry.

Drip torches

Smoke jumpers are being dropped by parachute close to the heart of the fire.

In an emergency, this portable shelter can be used by a firefighter as a last resort. Its metallic panels reflect heat. When the shelter is sealed, there is enough air inside to keep the fire-fighter alive until the fire has passed.

ED PULASKI SAVES IDAHO

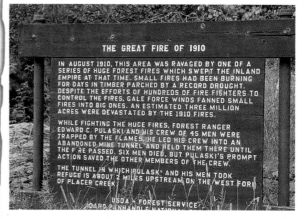

THE GREAT FIRE OF 1910

IN AUGUST 1910, THIS AREA WAS RAVAGED BY ONE OF A SERIES OF HUGE FOREST FIRES WHICH SWEPT THE INLAND EMPIRE AT THAT TIME. SMALL FIRES HAD BEEN BURNING FOR DAYS IN TIMBER PARCHED BY A RECORD DROUGHT. DESPITE THE EFFORTS OF HUNDREDS OF FIRE FIGHTERS TO CONTROL THE FIRES, GALE FORCE WINDS FANNED SMALL FIRES INTO BIG ONES. AN ESTIMATED THREE MILLION ACRES WERE DEVASTATED BY THE 1910 FIRES.

WHILE FIGHTING THE HUGE FIRES, FOREST RANGER EDWARD C. PULASKI AND HIS CREW OF 45 MEN WERE TRAPPED BY THE FLAMES. HE LED HIS CREW INTO AN ABANDONED MINE TUNNEL AND HELD THEM THERE UNTIL THE FIRE PASSED. SIX MEN DIED, BUT PULASKI'S PROMPT ACTION SAVED THE OTHER MEMBERS OF THE CREW.

THE TUNNEL IN WHICH PULASKI AND HIS MEN TOOK REFUGE IS ABOUT 2 MILES UPSTREAM ON THE WEST FORK OF PLACER CREEK

USDA - FOREST SERVICE
IDAHO PANHANDLE NATIONAL

In August 1910, many firefighters lost their lives in a great fire in Idaho.

One particular group was trapped when the wind changed direction. Forest ranger Edward C. Pulaski led them to an abandoned mine where they were able to shelter. His quick thinking saved many lives.

Taken from *The Blazer*, August 7, 1910

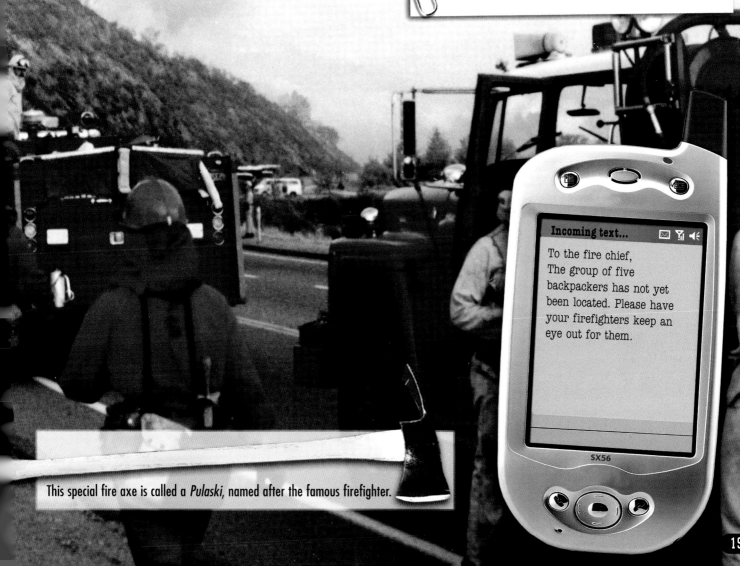

This special fire axe is called a *Pulaski*, named after the famous firefighter.

Incoming text...

To the fire chief,
The group of five backpackers has not yet been located. Please have your firefighters keep an eye out for them.

SX56

DAY 5—Late Afternoon
Location: *The road back to Upper Town*
The plan to contain the fire didn't work! The wind has increased. Flying embers from the crowns of the burning trees blew over onto the alignment points. Now, the fires are raging along the edges of Great Peak. There is nothing anybody can do to stop them. The most the firefighters can do now is prevent the fire from spreading out of its predicted path.

The fire crews have been pulled out of the most dangerous areas. There is no point in risking their lives when there is no hope of success. We are heading back to town.

Tanker planes have been brought in. They are dumping chemicals on the surrounding vegetation to slow the fire. The chemicals are brightly colored so that the treated area is visible from the air. This way, the pilots do not waste chemicals by bombing the same area more than once.

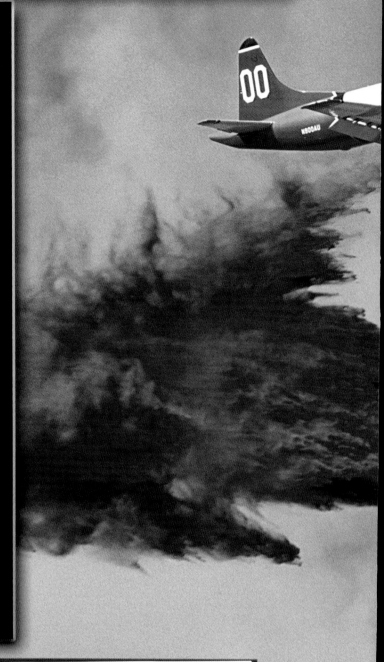

UNDERSTANDING FIRESTORMS

A firestorm is a dangerous phenomenon. The intensely hot air from a fierce fire generates a strong convection current in the atmosphere. A convection current is a column of hot air that rises so quickly that it sucks air in at the bottom, pulling in more debris to add fuel to the fire. Convection currents can even topple fire engines and suck firefighters into the blaze.

burning debris fills the air

debris sucked in from wide area

debris sucked in from wide area

strong updraft caused that sucks in ground level air

This helicopter is using a bucket to scoop water from the reservoir and drop it onto the fire.

FIRES SCORCH FAR EAST

Tropical rain forests are not usually known for wildfires. But, in 1997, a drought struck Indonesia and Malaysia. People began burning trees to clear more land for temporary agriculture. As a result, wildfires spread, leaving southeast Asia covered in smoke for months.

Taken from *The Blazer*, September 1, 1997

DAY 5—NIGHT

Location: *Shelter on the edge of the forest*

We are letting the fire burn overnight. Teams are still out there clearing fire breaks with the controlled burning method. They are working along the sides of the alignment areas. The wind is changing directions. The situation map needs to be redrawn. The team is still using the three points of analysis, which are weather (the easterly wind and the local wind in the valleys), topography (the slopes of the two peaks and the ridge), and fuel (the forests of the valleys and brush of the hilltops.) If the fire leaves its current alignment area and moves eastward, the hills above the towns will be more vulnerable. Several alignment points have been identified there.

Helicopters are out searching for the missing hikers. They are using powerful spotlights, but the smoke is so intense that the pilots do not have much hope of success.

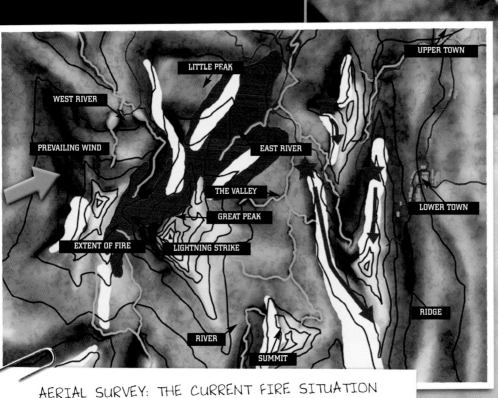

AERIAL SURVEY: THE CURRENT FIRE SITUATION

Map labels: UPPER TOWN, LITTLE PEAK, WEST RIVER, PREVAILING WIND, EAST RIVER, THE VALLEY, LOWER TOWN, GREAT PEAK, EXTENT OF FIRE, LIGHTNING STRIKE, RIVER, SUMMIT, RIDGE

REVISED POINTS OF ALIGNMENT MAP

The situation map is being revised. The firefighters have identified three more alignment points on the Ridge. The local winds along the Valley could likely produce uncontrolled fires dangerously close to Upper and Lower Town. The townspeople need to be alerted.

RAGING FIRE HITS AUSTRALIA

In February 1983, a drought coupled with unpredictable winds caused brush fires to blaze out of control in Victoria, Australia. Flames moved at an unstoppable rate, and smoke prevented effective evacuation. As a result, 71 people died.

Taken from *The Blazer*, February 3, 1983. This is what we are facing here.

Incoming text... ✉ 📶 🔊

Hi. This is the team back at the fire chief's office. We have received reports that smoke is reappearing down by the river where we thought the fires had been extinguished. You should make your way down there as soon as you can.

SX56

DAY 5 - Morning

Location: *By the river near Lower Town.*

The wind shifted overnight. The fire chief hoped that the fire had stopped at the banks of the East River, where it was burning itself out. It has reignited, though, and this time the tree crowns are burning. Before, moisture in the crowns kept the trees safe from the fire. Now, nearby fires have dried the crowns, making them flammable. The large flames have spread the fire wider, causing spot fires in unpredictable places. The fire has reached the alignment points on the ridge, and Lower Town is now threatened.

Because fires are uncommon in this area, residents have not taken care of their properties as they should have. Instead of burning trash regularly, as people are supposed to do in this region, homeowners have let the trash collect in their yards. The long period of drought has made this area very dry and hazardous.

Populations threatened by brush fires are usually evacuated as a precaution. Temporary housing is set up. Sometimes, it takes a while before people can return to their homes.

As the fires sweep along, they destroy all the temporary homes and poorly-built buildings. Stronger homes have a better chance of withstanding the fires.

DAY 6
Location: *Centre of Upper Town*

At last, the fire is under control. The fire department was able to contain the fire on the ridge, and it spread no farther than the predicted alignment areas. Because Lower Town is a new community, it has plenty of new roads, allowing vehicles to get close to the blaze.

Then came the other good news. The missing hikers are safe! When they saw that the whole area was going to be engulfed in flames, they took refuge in the railway tunnel at the head of the valley. They walked into the police station in Upper Town early this morning.

Now, it is important to stay alert. Although the fires seem to have burned themselves out, the fire chief is organizing a group of firefighters to keep watch so that the fires do not flare up again.

I drew this cartoon of the fire chief with Sparky the Squirrel. Everyone worked together to put the fires out.

MONSTER FIRE ON ITS WAY IN 2035?

Recently, the U.S. Forest Service made an alarming prediction. Experts suggest that the climate is becoming drier with longer periods of drought. By calculating the increasing areas of forest and brush that are likely to burn, the U.S. Forest Service estimates that a vast, uncontrollable fire will occur around the year 2035.

The fire chief handed me this newspaper clipping. It looks like we can't relax just yet.

Taken from *The Blazer*, December 1, 2003.

Computers and equipment greatly helped the fight against fire. Computers predict the fire's movement. Powerful machines like bulldozers and helicopters support the firefighters' efforts. Without this technology, fires could rage on for weeks.

Outgoing text...

To the Principal of City School: I have just witnessed a wildfire. I have also seen that people, through carelessness or spite, are the main causes of fires in the first place. I have learned so much! I'll tell you all about it when I get home.

SX56

One year later, I received a request to return to Upper and Lower Town to report how they are today. As you can see, life has begun to return to normal.

TWO TOWNS RECOVER

A look at Upper and Lower Town in the aftermath of last year's brush fire with a special report by our junior reporter from the City School, Elaine Wilkie.

F ire is not our enemy. In fact, it is a very important force of nature. Fire keeps the forests healthy because it clears away dead material that accumulates on the forest floor. It opens up the canopy of leaves and branches, letting in sunlight, which increases the kinds of plants and animals that can grow and live there. Only plants that can tolerate deep shade are able to grow in forests where fires are suppressed.

In the grasslands, fire sweeps away old growth to make way for the new, and it returns nourishment to the soil. Since their growing stems are underground and are insulated from fire, grasses are able to tolerate frequent burning.

Although natural fires are beneficial to the environment, most people see any fire as undesirable. People

Fire lookout posts have been installed. Cameras send images to a base in Upper Town.

Firefighters in both towns, including smoke jumpers, are continuing to educate the public about wildfire prevention.

building houses in fire-prone areas tend to avoid starting any kind of fire at all. For instance, wildfires often occur in countries around the Mediterranean Sea where the climate is hot, and the summers are long. This climate also attracts people who are searching for new places to live or places to vacation. Naturally, when people build homes or luxury resorts, they do not want fires to destroy them, so they avoid fire at all costs. They do not realize that fire-prone areas need fire, and that periodic controlled fires are necessary to keeping the environment in balance. As a result of people's hesitance to burn, fields and yards collect flammable debris until they reach unmanageable proportions. Then, when a fire does start, the result is catastrophic. If small, naturally-occurring fires are suppressed, they will eventually produce large, disastrous fires.

It is for this reason that fire departments are in existence. The primary job of the department is to control fires, not to extinguish them. Firefighters do a great service to residents and to the environment. All fire departments employ firefighters who are heroes. Unfortunately, it seems people become heroes only when something goes wrong or someone is in danger.

Fortunately, the inhabitants of Lower Town are no longer in danger and are returning to their homes. They are now taking the proper precautions because they have seen how close a wildfire can come to their community. Now, new buildings are

No trees near house roof

Gas tanks and other flammable items at least 30 feet from the house

Chimney covered by a spark preventer

Wide driveways for emergency access

Well-marked exits from the neighborhood

A diagram of one of the new houses with the safety measures implemented.

being constructed according to strict fire department regulations. People are also modifying existing structures. Residents are following the fire department's recommendations concerning which plants are safe to grow and harvest. They are also making sure debris does not collect and become a potential hazard. They have learned their lesson.

Many fires are caused by carelessness. Campfires should be built on rocks or bare ground to prevent vegetation from igniting.

GLOSSARY

Arson The illegal act of deliberately starting a fire to cause damage.

Coniferous A tree that has cones and needles, such as a pine or a spruce. Coniferous trees tend to be very flammable because of the oils and resins that they contain.

Convection The movement of a substance such as air or water due to heat. The substance heats up. Becomes lighter, and rises. Cooler substances flow in at the bottom to take its place.

Crown The branches and leaves at the top of a tree.

Ecosystem A community of living things, together with their environment. Animals, plants, weather, land, and water are all part of an ecosystem.

Firebreak A gap in the forest that has been cleared of vegetation so that fire cannot cross it.

Firestorm A fire that has very high temperatures. In a firestorm, a column of hot air rises so quickly that it sucks air in at the bottom, pulling in more debris to add fuel to the fire.

Flammable Having the ability to burn. Flammable is the same as inflammable. The opposite of flammable is non-flammable.

Flashpoint The temperature at which something catches fire and burns. It is also called the "ignition temperature."

Ignition The temperature at which something catches fire and burns. It is also called the "flashpoint."

Inflammable Having the ability to burn. Inflammable is the same as flammable. The opposite of inflammable is nonflammable.

Insulator A substance that reduces or stops the movement of heat, electricity, or sound.

Latitude The distance between the equator and a point north or south on the earth's surface. This distance is measured in degrees. Low degrees of latitude are close to the equator, while high degrees of latitude are close to the poles.

Meteorologist A scientist who studies weather and the atmosphere.

Organic Having to do with or coming from living things. In its modern sense, it usually means a material grown without the use of chemicals. To scientists, even materials grown with the use of chemicals are still organic.

Peat Soil from a wet area that is made up of decayed plants. Peat can be used as fuel or a fertilizer.

Scavenge To find and eat dead animals or rotting plants. Most meat-eating animals scavenge from the corpses of animals already killed.

Sediment Any solid material that settles to the bottom of a liquid.

Shrub A woody, low-growing plant or bush.

Slash-and-burn A form of agriculture in which trees are cut down and burned to clear space for crops. When the soil becomes no good for crops anymore, the area is then cut down and burned.

Smoke jumper A firefighter who parachutes into a location that is difficult to reach.

Triangle of Fire The three conditions that must exist before a fire can ignite. First, there must be fuel or something to burn. Second, there must be oxygen. Finally, there must be heat. Firefighting involves attempting to control one of these factors in order to break the triangle of fire.

Undergrowth Low plant growth beneath and around taller trees.

Wildfire A raging, rapidly spreading fire that occurs in a rural area.

INDEX

A

aerial map 16, 22

air tankers 7, 20

alignment points 16, 24

animals 9

Australia 4, 23

B

bush fires 4, 5

C

Campbell Prediction
  System 16

campfires 10

Canada 4

causes of fire 4, 5, 11,
  13, 27, 28

Chernobyl 14

Chile 4

coniferous forests 5, 12

controlled fires 8, 15, 22

crown fire 15

E

emergency services 18

F

firestorm 20

fireboats 7

firefighters 6, 7, 12, 14,
  15, 16, 18, 19, 20, 27, 29

firefighting equipment 6,
  7, 10, 18

fire hydrants 6

fireworks 11

flammable material 4,
  10, 11, 14, 24, 29

forest fires 4, 5, 10, 11

fuel tempometer 17

G

grass fires 5

Great Fire of Chicago 6

ground fire 15

H

heat 4

I

Idaho 19

Indonesia 21

inflammable material (see
  flammable material)

lightning 11, 13, 14

M

Malaysia 21

Maquis scrub 5

Mediterranean 4, 5, 29

O

oxygen 4

P

Pernin, Rev. Peter 6

Peshtigo Fire 6

portable shelter 19

Pulaski, Ed 19

S

savannah 5

shadometer 17

Siberia 4

smoke jumpers 18, 19

South Africa 4

Sparky the Squirrel 10, 11

statistics 13

surface fire 15

T

The Great Barbecue
  (see Peshtigo Fire)

topography 22

U

Ukraine (see Chernobyl)

U.S.A. 4

W

water pumps 6, 7

wildfires (see also brush
  fires and forest fires)
  4, 5, 7, 8, 13, 15, 21,
  27, 28

wind gauge 17

Wisconsin 6

Yellowstone National Park
  8, 9